GW01162555

# Love Letters

C S Lind

*To JT, Vessel and the lady at the grocery store, who I promised I would dedicate something to.*

# Love Letters

*All alone!*
*Whether you like it or not,*
*Alone is something*
*you'll be quite a lot.*

Dr Seuss

**CONTENTS**

RED			1

BLUE		107

YELLOW	189

# RED

I just wanted to say
I remember the time
We lay on your bed in silence
The air was thick
The sheets were sweaty
You looked me in the eyes
And did not look away
Until all the suns had set
All the waves had crashed
The stars had burnt out
My bones had all broken
It was the closest we have ever been
And I had never felt so far away from you

*- you were my wonderland and my nightmare*

You bit my lips to blood
I could not pull away
Your cigarette smoke did not wash
Out of my hair for days
I still feel your bedsheets under my fingers
And the tears I cried in the shower
I have prayed a thousand times
That god will make you cower

Set the sorrow in stone
The reaper is my soulmate
I let you cut off my circulation
Just to go on a date with him
I bleed and burn
To catch a kiss
Ache and suffer just to watch him undress

*- fine line between pleasure and pain*

loving you was
a ballad about heroin,
the smell in the air right before rain,
and a favourite song, ruined by a sad memory.

I didn't tell you when you said her name wrong
I decided it sounded better as a creation of your tongue
Flawless, intoxicating and perfect
Just like everything else you did

I wish I could tattoo your kisses onto my skin
Your lips belong to the devil
And my heart is owned by sin
The world is on its knees for you
Trembling hands on heartbreak addicts
Warm souls, lined up on cold platters

Get me high and call me baby,
Tell me I'm not mean,
The need to feel eats me alive,
Can't cope with this in between.

She creates chaos, holds fire in her eyes,
Flirts with death, for he does not despise.
Sends her roses, red as blood, leaves bruises on her thighs.
I want to watch the colours change, I want to kiss them better,
She will never realise that my mind is her love letter.
Black lace and silver chains,
Rip me apart and fill me with pain,
A torture I would beg for, if she only could see
Anything beyond her constant, aching need to flee.
I swear she's got *devilish* tattooed on her tongue,
Fascinator, manipulator, a shame that now she's gone.

You know I crave regret
I wonder how many lies I have to tell
To get you addicted

Flowers bloom in my blood
A creature of filth
Rising from the flood
Do you think that you could hurt me?
'Cus I wish that someone would.

How magical
How powerful
She must be
To be a slut when she wants you
And a slut when she does not.

Your lips burn on my skin,
Your name branded into my neck, letters sharp and thin.
Plagued by foreign tastes that won't leave my tongue,
The sound of your heartbeat reminds me that we're young.
The smell of your shirt is stuck in my hair,
Dirty cigarette smoke floats in the air,
So much evidence of love,
Waiting for a sign from above,
Constant prayers for a conviction, pleading for a sentence,
You're heaven, and I'm at the gates, begging you for entrance.
At least I can count on stolen kisses to forever haunt me,
While the gods play and burn and taunt me.

You would never let him lay a hand on you,
Mock you, cut you, tear you apart.
You would scream to heaven if he sliced you open,
And yell out if he hurt your heart.
So why do you do it to yourself?

the love will hurt
and the guilt will kill you
the love will hurt
and the guilt will kill you
the love will hurt
and the guilt will kill you
the love will hurt
and the guilt will kill you

How fast do these tears fall, in comparison to the entire universe?
Dirty face, messy hair.
Wish you were high tonight, but the walls would stare,
And your parents are already disappointed, for the ways you use.
He says he'll run away and hide with you,
But somehow it just doesn't seem true.
And as much as I hate to admit,
I'd like to have your name, keep it for myself,
Cut it into my skin with needle and ink, like a trophy on a shelf,
No one else could have it, and no one else could see,
A tiny dirty secret, the same way you see me.

I flew to the other side of the country
To spend a few days loving myself
But you danced in my mind
All day and all night
You know I love the way you hurt me
A living, breathing wreck,
So, do it again, I dare you, babe, snap my fucking neck.

Our pain is pleasure
Our god is dead
Our love is wretched
And it's all in your head
I don't want to wait for the other side
Take it all, I'll bleed for you
Growing pains, but no more pride
Ready to drown and deaf from thunder
The only place we belong together is 6 ft fucking under

If my mistake is loving too hard
I don't want to learn
I don't know where I'm going
But I know that you'll be there
My pulse is yours, check your wrist
I've had enough pretending
Hand around my throat tighter
Make my head lighter
So I can't see all the flaws
And I'll love you again

<u>massacre of intimacy</u>

Poetry and pornography, baby
Blood stains on my jacket
Haunting me
You're rotting in my hands
Been so scared of love and how it's never planned
It's going to kill you
And when it does
I'll use my imagination
To see what it's like
To be enough again.

I had almost forgotten the name of your street
But you answered the phone
Because you thought I might have been in trouble
I am not sure how to tell you there was no need for concern
Until I heard your voice again.

<u>I hate Tallai</u>

Lucky me or crazy you?
Still taste amazing bruised
Poisonous, damaged
When would be a better time?
Thank you for the venom
You are a storm in skin
A lethal injection they all beg for in the end

I wish I could forget
The haze behind your eyes
The drawings your broken hands can't make
And all the rushed goodbyes
The taste of rum on your tongue
When did our fire die?

<u>Tax time</u>

Sentient scum, bad dreams, anonymous club
A plethora of things that Should Not Be
He doesn't care if you don't go to the pub
Sugar lips and candy hearts
I hope you're not in love

Divine violence
A love shared by strangers
Lost again, faceless
Tell me what you want
We don't have time for romance

I saw an article titled
*The Saddest Words In The English Language*
But the author had clearly never heard
The way my name sounds leaving your lips

Chapped lips and rough hands,
You've got bloody knuckles from killing time
You tell me you're hypnotised
I'm suffocating in your huge bedroom
Freezing cold in your arms, despite the heat
And, god, I hate these cityscape sheets
You are in love with that girl we know,
With the long hair and faded tattoos
Tell myself it's meant to be, and I'll do it all again
With the next person who holds me tight now and then

<u>Sympathy for the Devil</u>

Always need soap ready
To tell you how I'm feeling
Wash my mouth out, clear the crime scene
Hand me down
Passed around
Look what you did
Back from the grave, to tell you I love you
Hell is easier to live with, so far through
Didn't lose my mind, left it in your sheets
But honestly, I'd rather set it on fire in the streets

give me a reason
for the dread in my mind
stand at the foot of my bed
pistol in your fingers
point it at my head
lean on the dresser
burn me with your stare
break the skin
you're witch hunting
a casualty of you
radio interference, misadventure
you make my world so blue

## I'd Do Anything For You To Tell Me We're Done Again Because My Memory Has Gone Blurry And I Need To See You

maybe you should get "that's my damages to deal with" tattooed on your fucking face
then you wouldn't have to say it every time you don't want to take the blame for your mistakes
cause when I drink I miss you so much, god, it makes me ache
wish I could hear you blame me for our problems, those memories are erased
I'll even leave the door unlocked, baby, just in case.

I would like to write a love song
about the way your voice sounds when you're falling asleep
even though I cannot sing
I would tell the whole planet how your hands feel in mine
when we talk at the top of the hill
until the sun comes up
and how it doesn't shine as bright as you, even first thing in the morning.

If I get a little prettier will you love me?
You never even told me why
I don't sleep much anymore
When I do your face is all that I see
That's not the way I thought it would be
When I imagined love as a child
I wonder when I decided to settle
And we decided to choose pain over nothing.

the city is dead without you
the waves do not crash
mutilation,
mass murder,
genocide.

not everyone will get out alive.

I told them I was scared now
they said maybe it was for the best
because if I was scared
I wouldn't get into any more trouble

I need you to care
and I still taste the cigarettes on his breath
and it screams in my skull when I drive past his street
I have nightmares now
the scars on my skin are all I can see
none of this body belongs to me

I read about her body and it made me cry for mine
She wrote of tight skin and mountains
But all I have is medication, midnight calls
And holding hands under the table
At that restaurant with the red vinyl seats

crying
are you high?
he sleeps beside me
and he breathes so loud
and I hate who I have become
powerless
poisonous
picturesque
hard to kill

A thousand paper cranes wouldn't make me love you
A ring of salt is not protection enough
Forgive who you were before
Memorise the curve of her back
Flowers at the end of the world
Lost in the devil's playground
Find me in your bad dreams
Knew I would never know you
A nihilistic vessel
A shitty interlude
Tasting of cherries and whiskey

<u>a projection of my heart onto the ceiling like a theatre</u>

rum burns my throat
and I think about how you are the most beautiful person I know
I lay awake trying to figure out the moment it changed
playing back every second in my head
I told my doctor about you and the colour of your eyes
and the way bruises and blood felt a small price to pay
for you to open up to me
to listen to your stories
and not fall asleep until after you already had

Your touch like rose petals
Your eyes like a dream
Your voice is asphyxia
I am never clean

The body count is too high
To handle on my own
Do you ever look in the mirror and wonder
Where all of your love went?
Sometimes I think that guilt is the blood
That keeps me alive,
The same way I feel alone when I'm in a room with you.

If hurting me felt as good for you
As it does for me
In the bathroom at 3am
Then I can understand
Why you couldn't stop doing it.

Bite the hand that feeds
I can't love you how you need
The volleyball net took her to heaven
Thinking of sad things when she touches herself
My heart is a vulture, feasting on pain
Because nothing else feels the same
Nightmares just a fetish
Miserable, possessed
And weaker than before
A long, hellish, unending war

Sometimes god puts me into a snow globe
And I can see everything and entertain everyone
But I can't do the tricks unless they shake me
And they're all deaf to my screaming
I get so confused that I start to believe
The tiny world of drowning is my home
And I wish you could have seen me when I was happy

a fetishization of recklessness and pain
a personification of fear
a pile of pills, lipstick and a tight dress
mind-altering
spellbinding

*- femme fatale*

You were even prettier in the sun,
golden galaxies in your eyes.
You told me you would marry me
in 80/100 lifetimes.
What a shame, that in this one,
luck was not on our side.

When it comes, it suffocates
There is nothing else
It deafens and drowns
When it comes, it pushes
There is nothing else
It tears and claws
When it comes, she screams silent
And there is nothing else
Just another feeling she thought she had left behind

On the first birthday that you were drunk without me,
I heard the whole world shake
I was so uneasy that my back ached.

The lump in my throat was still growing-
gestation, incubation,
a new limb for each special day you spent without me.

Heartbreak does not seem to end
the world still finds a way to remind me of you
and the way you tasted on a Saturday night.

I almost wish I was full of hate,
because I think it would be easier
than this state
of being simply and completely
without you.

*- October 21*

love is a merciless knife
logic is a swift hand
and guilt is the salt in my wounds.

it's a warning
get out while you can
she'll eat you alive
and claw you to pieces
without even knowing
her name in your flesh
and after she exhausts you
brain, blood and bone
she will beg
that you don't go

A desire to be sedated
My heart has been defaced
Soft skin sliced to ribbons
Letters to razor blades.

You are the highest flood
I cut myself trying to pick up the pieces of your heart.

there's a fine line
between hate and love
when you're in the room
I feel all of the above

you make me so sad
the heavens and the angels weep
when they look down on us and see
the company we keep
when you are away my body is cold
and when we are together
I exist as raging thoughts and melting gold

*- the only thing I can rely on you to do consistently is bring me down*

so foolish of me
to forget how committed you are
to pushing away
anyone who makes the mistake
of seeing beauty
when they look at you

so desperate to prove them wrong

In your car
Smells like home
Soft humming noises
Distracted by the moon
Keep your eyes on the road
I'll steer for you, but can't focus for long
Blood on the windows
Mud on the floor
I'm forgetting how to breathe
Please open the door

I feel you falling
and I drown in guilt
now you are an accomplice -
a witness,
*involved* -
in the tragedy of my mind

<u>Friday</u>

No one knows you like I do
Bruises on my neck
Stains on my favourite jumper

My heart is full of love for you
But my head knows what those hands will do
Your god complex is like a star to follow in the night
But it won't lead me to paradise

The darkness pulls me closer
You only want me cus I'm mad
And I'm only pretty when I'm sad

I do hope you teach your children different

I remember asking a god I didn't believe in
Why I gave you so much of myself
To see if he knew
But he just shrugged and went on
Painting the sky
The colour of your eyes
Slimming the gap between heaven and hell

I loved you, and you did not.

He carved words into my ribs
A reason for the pain
His name burning inside each time I breathe
Something to keep my mind from going silent
Nothing more than a prisoner

You bloom while I decay

DO NOT STOP TAKING THIS MEDICINE ABRUPTLY

(maybe you should have come with a warning)

You made me cry
You made me ache
And now I'm different
And you're the same

A hard pill to swallow.

You live in my head.
There is a bookshelf filled with bibles
And all the porn your heart could desire.
But you spend your days screaming out the windows
Hissing and shouting
And you don't stop
Until you see blood.

It's been a while
How have you been?
You make my head pound
But, old friend, you know I've always had trouble,
When asking you to leave.
You write me love letters,
Harsh lines on the page like the scars on my thighs
But we both know you're a liar.

*they tell me it's bad, but not how to escape.*

I could list a million songs that I am certain were written about your eyes,
(even that one about the girl in Illinois)
I save them all to playlists, tiny pieces of my heart.
I switch them into order
Tell the history of us
But I never listen
Because I'm still hoping the story isn't over yet
And you know how I hate starting something I cannot finish,
Just the opposite of you.

Ethereal
Twin flames
Always searching for someone else to blame
Cutthroat lust, laced with bad intentions
A bottle of rosé
Stronger as strangers, but cannot stay away
Kisses down my shoulder blades
Trying to love someone who is not there
Is like trying to survive without clean air
It feels so dark inside my body
I am so scared you will break the hearts of all your sons
God ends when we are in the same room
A film you'll watch again even though you know the characters are doomed

sometimes I cry until I can't anymore
until no noise comes out
until my head is thumping
and I wish you could see
what you have done
and feel the pain that I feel
that never leaves me
with every step I take with heavy feet
and every breath I steal
from someone more deserving

*the smell of my own blood*
*reminded me of your tongue*
*pushing its way into me*
*without asking*
*without checking*
*without permission*
*the copper taste*
*the stains*

rape.

she's made of gunpowder
and wilting roses
sitting shyly
in empty vodka bottles

your voice is warm caramel
your touch, barbed wire
the way you threaten me is hot coffee on a cold night
and the feeling of your hands around my throat
is an answer to my prayers

it's starting to hurt a bit more than I can handle
we don't have a safe word for love

how do I still see you every day?
the barista with the jacket,
and that actor has your nose,
the drunk man across the street
is walking the same way you do
I wonder if he's heading home to hurt someone

sometimes it is loud and rough and raw
to feel as if someone else is there
reason to put on a show
not quite so alone

I have done it again
and like the night, it never ends
crawling into my mind
slow and grotesque,
like an arachnid with missing legs

I have done it again
and we lose the battle
love is like war,
declared by the bored
and left to burn out

I have done it again
the birds in the morning
will send me to sleep
and the rising sun
will make me weep

I have done it again.

finished that bottle of rum tonight
dancing around the house alone
you know you made my heart hurt
but I have to tell myself you didn't realise
because I don't know how to see you as anything but perfect
and I don't understand how you could break things so easily

I can't even say you make my chest hurt
because there is no you anymore
just memories
and a ghost
no good excuse for the lump in my throat
as far as my dogs know, you do not exist
your hands on my steering wheel have disappeared by now
and I gave you back the dirty t-shirt
remnants gone
it doesn't seem fair that you will not ever fill my lungs again
your smell is a lyric from a song I cannot quite put my finger on

The world belongs to you
And the rest of us are just here
For your entertainment
But one day, you'll be treated
The way you've treated all of us
Do you think you could handle that pain?
Because I fucking doubt it.

I know people say it is unlikely out of billions that you are the one
out of islands and countries and oceans
but your family is made up of someone from everywhere
so, does it not make sense
to feel
that they travelled worlds
to get here
to bring you to me

Do you pray to him?
Do you talk about me?
Spill secrets of sweaty sheets,
And sick whispers seeping into your skull?
Do you tell him how Time was gone?
How she left us on that beach
And all we had
Was to watch the blood,
Falling slowly into the sand?

Repent, confess
Forget everything that makes you burn
Chemicals and contusions
Every time you found a way to tell yourself
That it meant more

*October:*

I am beginning to entertain the concept that my love may not be a weakness.

There are bruises on my windpipe
I feel them when I breathe
There's so much hurt I'll let you give
In the hopes that you won't leave.

He sang of the way drunk kids love.
Do you remember the time we cried?
In the middle of that field
With fire and laughing all around us,
Because we were both so in love.
Do you remember later that night?
Even the sky was overwhelmed
By how hard our hearts belonged to one another
That she cried as well
And we rushed for cover
Hoping her tears did not flood our tents?
But it was okay really,
Even if the fire went out,
Because we had each other.

your quiet eyes and scarred stomach
have broken something
I thought you would fix

Hands are broken from fighting
Teeth are fucked from taking hits
Don't think I've seen you without your lip split
Gave you everything you needed to destroy me
On a silver platter with doilies and candy
But all I learnt
Was that there was someone more scared of love than I was.

If lust is a sin
Send me straight to hell,
Because the things I want to do to you
Would make angels cry

How could you leave when you knew it was dark inside?
Did you ever tell your therapist about me?

a hundred warm bodies
a hundred heavy breaths
a hundred hearts to fall for
a hundred messy deaths

and once they're all gone
crushed fine, like cocaine on the edge of the sink
the music distorts, the dust settles,
I am in another world
and infinitely more convinced
that your name belongs cut into my skin,
only leaving me to be without you, in the moments that I
decay.

I missed you
so much to say
set the words on fire
no talking, only touch
dance with me forever.
I see your smile in the smoke surrounding me
I don't want to drive away again
late breakfasts at shitty cafés
you've lost your shoes and I've ripped my stockings
but we almost feel like we used to

I'm all you fucking dream of babe
mascara running down my face
innocent eyes and nasty smiles
fucking pixie dream girl

<u>decay</u>

rot with me, baby
fear life, not death
hold me tight
push me hard
love me so much it's perverted
I am scared of the crazy inside me
but I don't mind it if you're psycho too
tell me more lies, tell them crueler
you know it makes me swoon
say you'll end it now, before you hurt me
and then stay forever
darker the bruises, the more you adore me

rot with me baby
but let me inside at 2am
kiss me rough before I'm even in the door
this is no time for romance, lover
cry to me, ache to me, focus
tell me you're out of your fucking mind,
you know it'll make me stay
ask me how I pray
for god to fix you
hold me when I need to leave,
just to make sure I stay drunk off of your scent

rot with me baby
you're here when I'm alone
the dirty sheets, the slowest songs
why did you hold my hands every time?
the way I feel is disgusting
and if I could wish,
it would be for you, just a little closer

rot with me baby
and when you're finished being filthy
you can tear the heart right out of my chest
things are getting a little tight in there anyway
and I am ever so pretty when I cry

I died today
but you are always welcome back
I am sure I will be here,
cold, numb, waiting
it will end in blood and tears
and I will beg you
to do it again.

Sick and disgusting
Filthy and vile
Maybe you'll change your mind
Because I'll still be here
And as much as I hate to say it
I'll do anything you ask
At any time, in any state of mind
I'll be here
Ready for you
While you're fucking and drinking and loving
You know I'll move mountains to make you smile
Nothing I wouldn't do
To breathe your disease one more time

You could put a gun to my head
And I would lean closer
And tell you to pull the trigger
Just to see that look in your eyes again

people will walk out
and they owe you nothing
even if your heart beats for them
and they smell of roses

not completely human anymore.

the most terrifying part comes,
when you realise you can't run anymore,
forced to feel all you fear,
even though all that fills your mind
is venom he would spit.

nobody does it like you do, babe

bite me so hard it burns
you are filth
and I am scum
and we belong together
kisses like razors in your mouth
he is a gun
we are only "we" alone in this bed.
do you think they'll notice if I disappear?

our mistakes make us who we are
and I'm proud to say that my mistake was loving,
all you are is someone who makes lovers cry.

I hope my makeup stained your jacket
the way your fingers left marks on my soul

violent
vulgar
red
running
you have killed her
and nothing remains
not one un-tied shoelace
or a razor-sharp glare
not even the smell of her flowery shampoo

the later it gets,
the messier my thoughts sound
laced together
like a daisy chain
or an overdose

sad hours.

City sounds
Hot breath
Fingers bruising thighs

Dirty sheets
Fingertips
Street lights
Cold eyes

Why does she run so far?

I yell and I scream
And my drink is too big for one hand
And my heart is too small for all this love
And you've got me wrapped around your finger
We could capsize boats with this feeling

I sat naked on your couch
Wrapped in a musky sheet
The ghosts of the night flooded my lungs
I wondered if you could feel them too

The marks on my neck from her nails
And the cuts in my lips from the sun
She coughed blood
It dripped blue and black
I watched the threads keeping her together fall
The space between us grew like a forest fire

I would throw away this library in my mind,
Cut deep into my veins,
To make you see the light.
Tear my heart out
And serve it to you with tea,
To show you that you're not alone.

I saw your face in my window last night
I think they put my heart 6 feet deep
So you wouldn't get lonely
I wish they'd asked me first, invited me to go along,
When you fell.

I wish I was included
When the glass shattered along with your bones.

I wish I'd kissed your cold lips
Before the dirt made its way under your hard nails,
Before the worms dug into your soft skin
And took you away from me.

I am so full of love,
I only want to give it.
I am so full of hope,
So why do you keep leaving?

He said thought I was nicer when we first met.

# BLUE

you were a ghost when I met you
already hopeless
already gone
something possessed me
thought I was god
but even the power of the heavens
couldn't fix the devil in you

I can't give you what you need
I hope I don't break you, I hope you still believe
I love you with all of my soul
But it's not the love you need

you acted like our love was god
but when I prayed
all I heard
were my own words,
the world echoing back to me
my wishes were the same as those of the stars
because you left us all so confused
that even the sky needed to scream for help
looking down for answers
when I looked up in search of the same thing.

I don't remember what nights used to be like
Before him
I don't know how to sleep anymore
I don't get to decide when it's time for bed,
My eyes burn and my stomach churns
I don't remember what nights used to be like

*-another choice he took from me.*

please leave the light on
split knuckles and a busted lip won't lead me home
blood dries like dirty crystals
bubbles thick and slow,
intimate and erotic
I feel you touching me
when the copper fills my lungs
they burn and ache
I can't stop running
carnal and vulgar
fucking grotesque
desires that will end in tears
needles in your eyes and your mouth taped shut
pick at the holes in my skin
decide how you will destroy it all
figure out how you want me

I cannot see you.
I close my eyes, deep breaths.
I ask the clouds to rain, so the sounds will drown out my mind
But the memories still deafen me
I remember suffocating.

I cannot see you.
A buzzcut.
An earring.
A tattoo of *HELL* on your knee,
Maybe heaven, trying to warn me.

I cannot see you.
I do not know the colour of your eyes
I do not know what your bathroom looks like
A record collection under a gathering of empty lighters.
Small green lights strung under the window.

I cannot see you.
A mirror I had wished wasn't there.
Ironic really, that I was still wishing at that point
Still thinking that there was a god to help me,
When he didn't even give you a face in my memories.

I left that night and my body is still waiting for me to come back.

you held me and said
that there was no one else
not in all of this time
not in every sunset
the apology was raw
the kisses were rawer
the scratches will fade
but my heart will feel the same

## Thief

I don't sleep anymore
I've forgotten how to quiet my brain
From the white noise
I switched it to loud, to escape your touch
But now the button is stuck
It won't be quiet

When I get exhausted
I see you in my dreams
You are the blackest sky,
Or the oldest man,
Each form you take exists to rip me apart
I don't remember what the nights used to be like
I think that's what I'm most angry about
You took the dark away from me.

we are bored
and so
we love each other
vile and incongruous
a world run by maggots
drowning in dirt

I deserve better
I hope it haunts you, what you did to me
I hope you lay awake at night
Staring at the ceiling
Replaying it over and over
Until your blood runs cold
Until your hands shake
Until you forget how to breathe without focusing hard
And even then, every breath that enters you
Rushes to leave
Because the air knows what you did
And it is disgusted to be with you
But no matter how many times it runs
It will keep coming back
Because you always have to fucking be in charge of everything.

if water in my lungs is what you want
hold my hands behind my back
and push my head under,
and kiss my neck while you do it.

Does she know her parents are scared?
They talk in quiet voices when she leaves the room

We went to a lemon tree in a glowing garden
It asked us to write wishes
And all I wanted was happiness
But half an hour later I was crying
And that's sort of how I've felt, loving you.

how cold of you to hold me so tightly
night parties and neon lights
swimming pools and dirty nails
I would let you break my heart a million times over
he split your lip
and something changed in your eyes
and the noises and the warm light of the night became cold
and shallow
all I could see was you, looking through me

they took everything away
and when I thought nothing else could leave,
you did too

I sort of sit and wait for you
I am not sure why
My bedroom feels crisp and cold
Almost eerie
I try to figure out when you finish work
When you'll drive home
I wonder if I'm on your mind

I wonder what you'll say to me tonight
Your temper makes me scared

He says *You're drunk and rambling*
But I'm not that drunk
I let him think I'm wasted, bonkers, completely fucked
Maybe it's so I can get away with more
Maybe it's so he'll ask if I'm okay.

Nothing else exists,
Just street signs
And bright lights
And you in my head.

Don't lie
Don't say it ruined you
You were fucked up before this

I was really craving love
But I guess you will do

Young, filthy, insecure, don't bite those nails any further
Fuck his smile and the way he smells
Because he doesn't look at you
The way that he's supposed to

I want to forget every single detail of the walk we went on
what the plants looked like around the corner
or the way the wall felt against my shoulder blades when
you pushed me onto it
or the taste of your tongue
or the feel of your face against mine
and your fingers grazing my palm
and the way you moved the hair off my neck
so you could kiss warmth into my veins

I know nothing will compare to the rooftop feelings
and the way the red lights shined on your face
but every time I walk in the door
I expect to see you leaning on the railing
but every time, it's someone else
following me with curious eyes
the wrong stares
the wrong way
not yours
never yours

you're high out of your mind
I'm low out of mine
dropping and falling
caged like songbird with no tongue
redefining insanity
whispers early in the morning
stories filled with *if only* and *too late*

a monster
will love you endlessly
gritty and raw
disorderly and chaotic
won't let it hurt you
a heart here, if you ever need it
help yourself
take what you desire
and throw away what's left
it's no good for anything
but loving you.

it is not love if you tell him your thoughts are killing you
and he says he loves his girls a little crazy

time passes instantly or not at all
I put makeup on just to cry it off
chemicals burn in my eyes
the same way your second-hand love burns in my lungs

crack open my skull
all in my mind belongs to you

I press on the bruises you left on my chest
just to check I didn't make you up in my head

Soft skin and rough kisses
Salty hair and bare feet

You told me we would watch Snow White
I still haven't watched it
In case you come back

Nothing has tasted the way it should,
since you left.
No-one is warm enough.
No skin feels right,
pressing against mine,
the way yours did.

A friend of mine suggested I write you a letter
With all the things I wish I could have said
But there is not enough paper in the world
For me to fight this dread

I can never be who I was before you
I used to be trapped in this body
But now I have torn it apart
And there is nothing I want more
Than to be stuck where I was before

*lover* is a funny word
do you feel loved?
will my heart be free,
the day that I die?
or will you hold it in your hands,
even in death,
as it grows cold
and rotten?
when my eyes have left my skull,
eaten away by the elements,
will I still see your beauty?
when my skin caves in,
and bones push through,
hollow and dusty,
will I still be yours?

the world will swallow me up without you
I have to learn to breathe on my own
but something tells me that
resurrection is not a one-woman job.

*- it is okay to need help*

that song you like played in the shops today
pieces of my soul fell all over the dressing room floor
remember when I told you if I ever broke your heart, I'd
break my own heart too?

if you go,
I will become a ghost again.
when the music stops I hear the sea,
and she reminds me that I'm all alone.
it hurts more than that razor blade when you were sixteen,
more than falling from the tallest tree at your grandparent's house,
and once the pain slows down
it numbs me to the fucking core.

I will never understand why you were so afraid
Of letting me love you

I thought you were gone forever
You told me my eyes were so sad
I felt as if nothing could fix this
Not even a pain inflicted on myself,
Which used to fix everything

I am suffocating, silent.

Watching from behind my eyes
A spectator
As I left my heart
In your tiny bedroom
And walked out.

even the moon doesn't lie like you do,
and she's only ever shown me half of herself.

how am I ever not going to be in love with you?

I guess I am just confused
I thought that love was supposed to conquer
But so far it just makes my eyelids heavy and my heart tired

I feel you falling out of love with me
and I can't even make it poetic
I think I will drown in my tears
you are the only thing I've ever been certain of

I know your favourite colour
And your stupid middle name
You left me standing at the bus stop
Drunk and cold
Where do we go from here?

chemicals won't leave her be
a date to see the sunset at the beach
cried on the drive home
hot chocolate and sandy feet are nothing
but an OCD trigger when you're alone.

I could fuck the world
But all I wish for is you

I always hated rum and coke
something about your lips resting on the glass
made me ok with the taste.

funny how I write about the trauma
the same way I write about you.

hands all over my body as if you are afraid
I am going to disappear
and I don't blame you for the fear
but one day we will fall asleep
without wishing things were different.

you said you can tell where hair grows
because my skin is a different kind of soft
you said you don't mind me in the sunlight
I said I like it dark, just shapes and touch
silence is okay with you,
but we won't know the truth until it's too late

it's like I want to swim
I want to fall into you
asphyxiate

he told me he's going to leave soon
I thanked him for the warning
a formal interaction
with an ending already decided
no fight or fall out
not even a soft goodbye.

you promised to take me to the theme park
because I'd never been on a rollercoaster
even though promises make your head hurt
because of things you won't tell
you warned me you'll disconnect
because that's what you do to people
even though I care
because you're not good at this
and there is no pretty ending or revelation
it was ugly and horrible
you should've worshipped her sooner.

## Red Flags

you held me down
hands around my throat
kissed me hard
and hissed
*don't ever let me see you cry*

I can't spend another day in this house
he said he would look at me
and wonder who I was
because the girl he knew
had disappeared
her eyes were blank
and her stare lead nowhere
shaking hands
cold as ice
a shell in his arms
a carcass in the living room
I screamed from inside
but the sound wouldn't come out

Did I tell you I don't have to wash my hair when I leave your house?
Ghosts that have haunted me for my whole life
Aren't scared of the smell of your sheets.

I wish I could put these feelings into words
There is burning and choking
But not in the way we like it
My throat closes up at the thought of you
I nearly crashed my car last night
Your honey eyes have hurt me more than I could hurt myself
The care for my diet is low
But the appetite I have for you is disgusting
The fear for my wellbeing can be drowned in vodka
But the ache you cause in my heart only grows
The thing that hurts the most is that you left
Because you thought I was going to be the one to walk away
But everything about you made me want to stay

I told you no
You didn't care
You had sex with my body
I was not there

when I am with you, I become full
when you are with me, you become a ghost
who are you when you're alone?

- *Toxic*

Barely a ghost
Hardly a spirit
Reaching for something that isn't there
Lost even within myself
Faded tattoos and puffy eyes.

You do not have the time for me, and that is okay
It only tells me what a fool you really are,
To think that you *have the time* for anything,
Let alone to throw away a love this pure
It is okay though, I am not as daft,
I know I do not have the time to waste any more of it on you.

You showed me your heart, glowing and soft
And then you locked the doors and made me leave.
You asked me if I had been eating
And tattooing myself again.
I wanted to ask if fire still burns in your kiss,
Or if I'm supposed to run and hide,
When you push me away
But I smiled wide and told you
Everything was fine

*YOU NEVER FINISH ANYTHING.*

## Validity

Consensual sex doesn't make you cry in the shower.
Non-consensual sex does not exist, it is not sex, but violence.
All the facts I know
All the activism
Didn't change
That I had to see myself say
"I don't think it was rape enough."

Maybe if you had done it more or better
If you had been violent or loud
When I was trying to drive
Maybe if there had been someone around to see my face
Or the tears on the steering wheel when I drove home
Maybe I could tell someone and feel it means something.
"I don't think it was rape enough."

*- THERE ARE SO MANY LIES I TELL MYSELF TO SURVIVE*

I wish I was the terrifying force you saw before you knew me.
We were at the top of the world
And your hand was under me to stop the hand brake from digging into my back
And the saddest song came on
And I told you I thought it was pretty
And you told me I was pretty
And I wondered if it was only because I was sad.

My heart hurts from all of you
The love that almost was
The love that was ripped away from me
The love that you killed
The love that we grew like a garden
The love that was born from guilt
The love that hid in sadness
The love that happens so quickly and falls away just as fast
Both a blessing and a curse

everyone else says they ache for love
but I feel nothing
there's no screaming in my head
or burning in my chest
it's just silence
and cold hands
and a funny taste in my mouth
it is all so grey
without you here next to me

the doctor said it counts, what you did to me.
I said my recklessness came back on me,
my mum said karma doesn't work that way.
it stung when I scrubbed to get him off of me.
the tears burned and the water scalded.
I cannot connect the dots
even words don't belong to me anymore.

she carried the newspaper clipping with her
everywhere she went
the light has gone and it left without me

I still find myself hurting on your birthday each year
Maybe I'll ask someone if we can take February 21 out of
the calendar for good.

How can you still have your claws in me?
According to my 8th grade science teacher
Every single cell I am made of has died
And has been replaced by fresh ones now
How come even by becoming new
I cannot escape you

I am so tired
Of being tired
From the demons
And their claws
And their screaming
And the diamonds they use
To crush my lungs

I know it happened in the middle of the day
But in all my memories
The sky was the deadliest black
I wonder if she will one day explain herself to me

the pool is too hot
the pool is too cold
the water is burning me
where did you go?

I can never say it didn't happen,
I will always be someone else now
And I am terrified of that
But most of all
I am sorry I made you cry

<u>the first time I was scared of [leaving] you</u>

He told me I was glittering
And pushed his fingers through my hair
I could smell him
And the fast food in the back seat
And his arm was around me
And his hand was on mine
And his skin was glowing red from the radio lights
And I could feel his eyes on me
And the moon was blinding
And the clock said it was tomorrow,
But it was 3 minutes fast
And he kissed my hand and my cheek and then my hand again
And it would all have been so perfect
If I hadn't been so terrified of going crazy
The second I left that car

The only feeling worse
than always being second best
is watching yourself
fall
from
first.

When the night is quiet,
Except for the trees dancing in the wind,
I close my eyes
And I can feel
Where you took the blade
And cut your name into my skin

I miss holding you in the dark
your soft lips,
your gentle fingers,
moving slowly up my arm
the electricity when I feel you breathe on my neck
I think I am going to disappear

Sometimes I think
I deserve to be hurt
As badly as I hurt you
Over and over again
For each day that you stay

"who is it today?" he asks me.
he told me one night that he hates to phone.
he said he cannot stand it,
he doesn't know which me will greet him.
I realized he does not understand
that is how it feels
to wake up every morning
in this body.

Please tear me apart
I love you in such a way that I ache
I was the night
And you were the sun
Falling into me

Her hair was falling everywhere
It was no longer the colour of the sky
But none of her was
Although perhaps they matched at midnight.

The bath water was too hot
But if she focused hard enough, she couldn't feel it.

She scrubbed and scrubbed to make this body hers again
Maybe if she cut her nails
Turned the music loud enough
Maybe if she broke the mirror
Opened the windows
Screamed until there was blood

I don't think I come up from the downs
I just sit silent and get used to the sounds
I am asleep in my body
Asleep in my brain
Thin glass between us
The truth is hiding from me

sometimes I become am so unhappy
it is as if my entire being
is suspended above a flame,
burning like your breath on my skin

*Hanahaki Disease is a fictional disease in which the victim coughs up flower petals when they suffer from one-sided love.*

You took me to The Top Of The World
And threw up flowers at my feet
You lay it all out in front of me
And gave me everything
I think I saw an angel that night
And maybe it was the magic in the air
Or the warmth of your headlights
But I knew it was you
Always you

I miss you
- letters to myself

I saw you today
Your hair was thick and plaited
You didn't look happy or sad
You didn't look like anyone out of the ordinary
You were just someone else
Another stranger in the white noise of the supermarket
I only wish I didn't see you instantly
That I didn't remember every detail of your face
And the way your voice goes high when you get angry,
And throw your hands into the air
And the way you used to keep me alive

# YELLOW

I am home when I kiss you
I am yours and you are mine
Lips made of the clouds
Smile made of sunshine

you don't make me speechless
you fill me with the words I forgot I knew
and remind me of the beauty of language
I forgot to worship

You kissed me gently.
You kissed me so softly and carefully.
You kissed me with meaning.
I forgot how it feels to be treated like porcelain.
I forgot the love I deserve.

"Fuck…"
You smiled
"I've never seen anyone so happy about such shit weather."

how many times do I have to go to the vending machine
before you fucking kiss me?
the night is when its hardest
my heart pumping
late, disfigured, cadaverous
my thoughts thumping
painfully alive
disturbed, angelic, and anything but innocent.

*A compulsive need to be <u>more</u>.*

I still associate everything beautiful with you
even though I left
when I hear those songs
and drive past that street
and when the lights turn yellow
you are there
your eyelashes
your tears and blood and sweat and love
and someone is squeezing my chest

we were in the art gallery
and this room was dark
except for stars
and the sound of the sea played through black cubes
and we were alone
and you kissed me
and time did not exist

I want to feel powerful and pretty
but I want to be myself
I want to be small and soft
hold me
help me
love me when I can't do it on my own

Why do you fear love?
Why does intimacy make you shake?
I used to cry at the thought of wanting you forever
But I left it all too late
To tell you that the feeling changed.

I write so I remember how to feel when I forget.

You get to hear your voice every day.
I have to listen carefully when you speak to make sure I hear everything.
Then I play it back over and over, but the more times I spin the record, the more tired it gets.
Now the sound of your laugh in my head is just a memory of a memory, overplayed and faint.
What I wouldn't give to hear it brand new.

souls so young compared to the oceans and the trees
lovers loving
no one in this universe can hurt me,
as much as I can hurt myself.
the grass will stay green
and the water will keep running
and true love will be fleeting
and my mouth will keep tasting like you
and I guess we will learn to forgive.

More than anything I wish that I needed you.
I wish I didn't know I could survive.
Because knowing I don't need you
for my heart to keep beating,
my blood to keep running,
my eyes to keep seeing,
means all of this is want.
A craving.
An ache.
I won't die without you, but fuck, I wish that I would.

I wonder how you would feel if you knew
I got his smell on your shirt
And all of our love was buried in the dirt
Maudlin and quiet,
He's not the one who made time disappear.

even though I had to park the car
because I couldn't see past my tears
and your deodorant was on my jacket
the one thing I was sure about
was how powerful I was
when I discovered honesty
thick like honey, glowing like stars.

You in the morning.
You before bed.
Your hands around my waist when you kiss me.
Your fingers in mine, hands swallowing each other.
Drunk in my car, nervous at the pier.
Whistling so loud it echoed across the water.
Your eyes on my lips the entire time I talk.

Every now and again
When the night is black
The raging wind is white noise so loud
That it becomes silent
And she makes the mistake of tuning in
And she feels the love
So much
It burns her

forever reaching at each other
forever filled with storms and stars
I wonder if you are pushing for more
or truly happy with who you are
I do hope it is the latter

there is a thin layer of dust on my heart
soft in your fingers
but hurts your eyes
it's been a while since I let her play a part

no one is soft
no one is gentle
she grows tired

when I picture how you used to look
your face is stranger than ever before
and I realise I never knew you

Please be gentle, I heard she is trying to replace blood spatter on her skin with lipstick stains.

how did you make that sad song so happy?
remember how you protected me from the loud,
and when you pushed me on the swings at the beach
just before you pushed me up against your car?
your tongue was so warm and I could taste your gum
flooding my mouth

remember when I got drunk at your ex's house
and begged you to fuck me?
did I taste of raspberries?

remember when we went to the art gallery
for my birthday
and we cheered in the car
because I was 2 weeks clean?

And I know I should be loving someone
But I don't think it should be hurting this bad
I hope you can forgive me
For not knowing who I am
You got drunk and told me
I always want to die
I had a dream that I was drowning
I thought you would be the one to save me
But you were the one filling my lungs
So, I am not sad about the space between us
I think that's where it belongs

your laugh makes me believe we are made of stars,
of atoms that were once first kisses
true loves
hand holding
supernovas
soft breezes
new book smells
favourite songs
and sunshine

we used to go to the beach and I would cry in your arms
and we would watch the black sea
and remember how small we were
and the air was cold
and the moon was soft
and nothing was scary

Your voice sounds like a soft breeze
But it breaks me down like a fucking hurricane
I wonder how it is possible
That every being on earth
Does not feel their legs turn to jelly
And their hearts to fairy floss
When you walk into a room

if you treat him like god
he will become god
burning bridges, bruising souls
he will destroy everything
and at the end he will owe you no explanation
and it won't be your fault
but, fuck, it'll hurt.

when I lost you
my lungs collapsed
my eyelids burned
my bedroom numbed me
I did not breathe, or blink, or wiggle my fingertips
my brain shut off
leaving me with a default screen of your face
I found a ringing in my ears,
but upon closer examination
it was echoes of your laugh
I did not hear what my mother said
I did not feel the rain
I could not smell that fucking candle
Acomedown like cocaine.

I hope you can forgive me

I wonder if you know, that you are everything now
That the rain smells like you
The seawater tastes like you
That tingle in my tongue from the apple gelato
The light from the sun
The peace of the night

You don't get to be the person who hurts
And the person who heals
You don't get to kiss my cheeks
And hit them too
You don't get to bring me down
And then tell me you love me
You treasure me
Or you leave

Baby, baby, baby
Glassy eyes and cold fingers
Deafened by the sounds of the sea
Tell me pretty things
Baby let me read your lips

I don't know if this is love
But I listened to your favourite song
Before I went to sleep
Every night
For weeks.

We haven't talked since April
I see you everywhere
I see your shining reflection in places that you aren't
And I see your marks on new victims that you've found
I hope you know that you aren't coming back
And I hope I know so too

The beach never felt like home
Even after 18 years
Until you took me there one night
And we saw the moon
And wished for happiness
Now I am sure that I come from the sea.

*instagram - @cslind*
*cslind.books@gmail.com*

CPSIA information can be obtained
at www.ICGtesting.com
Printed in the USA
BVHW071115260219
541199BV00001B/132/P

9 780368 038518